written by
Nicole Asallas-Overman

FANSOME.

illustrations by **Moises Rameriz**

A true story about a little boy
with his very own style.

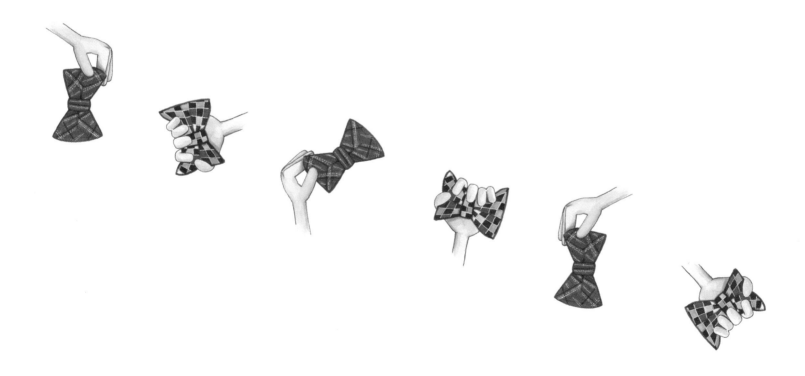

HI,
I'M ENZO.

THIS IS MY MOM.

SHE WORKS IN A FANCY PLACE.

THIS IS MY
DAD.

HE COACHES
BASKETBALL.

I LIKE TO HELP MY MOM GET DRESSED FOR WORK.

IT'S REALLY FUN
AND SO IS MY MOM.

SHE HAS SUPER FANCY SHOES.
SOMETIMES I GET SNEAKY
AND SLIP THEM ON WHEN
SHE ISN'T LOOKING.

I LIKE TO HELP MY DAD GET DRESSED FOR WORK TOO.

HIS BASKETBALL SHORTS FEEL SOFT AND SLIPPERY.

HIS SNEAKERS ARE EVEN BIGGER THAN ME!

ONE MORNING WHEN MY PARENTS WERE GETTING READY FOR WORK,

I HAD A REALLY GOOD IDEA!

I WAS GOING TO SURPRISE THEM.

I SNUCK INTO MY ROOM AND FOUND MY FANCY CLOTHES.

I SLIPPED ON MY BASKETBALL SHORTS AND BUTTONED UP MY SHIRT,

IT LOOKED A LITTLE STRANGE.

I GRABBED MY BRUSH AND WET IT WITH A LOT OF WATER. I REALLY LOVE WATER.

MY HAIR LOOKED JUST PERFECT

BUT SOMETHING WAS MISSING.

I ALMOST FORGOT MY
BOW TIE!

SUDDENLY, MY PARENTS WALKED IN.

MY MOM BENT DOWN, STRAIGHTENED MY BOW TIE

AND SAID,

"ENZO, YOU LOOK SO FANCY!"

THEN MY DAD WHISPERED

INTO MY EAR,

"SON, YOU LOOK SO HANDSOME."

JUST AS THEY STEPPED OUT OF THE WAY
I GOT A GLANCE OF MYSELF
IN THE MIRROR...

...THE END

Fansome @fansome_thebook

Follow these two childhood best friends on Instagram to keep up with their latest projects, passions and obsessions.

Author @naokidsbooks   Artist @moisesartnyc

PRINTED IN THE U.S.A.
www.nicoleasallas-overman.com

ISBN: 978-0-578-51968-5

One day my sweet 3 year old son asked me this very simple question.

"Mama, do I look FANSOME?"

It took me a few moments to digest his made-up word but once I realized
he was mixing the words FANCY and HANDSOME to describe his look I instantly
knew we had a message to share.

A tale of authenticity.

We as humans blend what we know and love
and with that we create our uniqueness.
We are all originals and that
is always something to celebrate.

My wish is that this story is
enjoyed by those of all ages
including you my dear Enzo.

Always with LOVE,

Nicole Asallas-Overman
Stylist
Wife
Mother
Author

This book is for you RPO

Thank you for always encouraging me, there is no greater gift than our little family.

XO

NAO

CPSIA information can be obtained at www.ICGtesting.com
Printed in the USA
LVIW011306071020
668195LV00018B/171